NEW ZEALAND

PICTORIAL

COOKBOOK

NEW ZEALAND
PICTORIAL
COOKBOOK

KOWHAI
PUBLISHING LTD

New Zealand's highest mountain 3762 metre Mt. Cook.

Published in 1992 by Kowhai Publishing Ltd.
10 Peacock Street, Auckland
299 Moorhouse Avenue, Christchurch.
Copyright © of recipes and food photographs is as indicated in the index. All recipes and food photographs without a credit are copyright © Jan Bilton.
Landscape photography copyright © Warren Jacobs Photography Ltd.

Design and finished art by John Burt Graphics, Christchurch
Printed in China

ISBN 0–908598–55–6

NEW ZEALAND PICTORIAL COOKBOOK

Food Editor

JAN BILTON

Co-ordinator

ELSA HAYDON

Landscape photography by

WARREN JACOBS

CONTENTS

Whanarua Bay, typical of many sheltered coves on the
eastern Bay of Plenty coast.

SEAFOODS

The clear, clean oceans around New Zealand are home for many species of fish and shellfish. Many are common to all coastal waters, however, most regions have their own specialities.

The western shores of Northland provide shellfish such as toheroa and tuatua although the former are now strictly protected. The seas off the coast of Northland and North Auckland provide recreational and game fishing as well as an income for commercial fishermen. Species of fish in this area include snapper, hapuku, barracouta, mackerals, hoki, gurnard, ling, yellowtail and squid. The shellfish include scallops, paua, rock lobster, kina (sea eggs) and clams.

Rock lobsters and scallops from the Firth of Thames are famous. This area has also developed large rock oyster and mussel farms. A speciality from Hawkes Bay waters are crabs. On the opposite coast off Taranaki the speciality of the area is squid (calamari).

Nelson's Tasman Bay and surrounding seas attract orange roughy, warehou, hake, hoki, squid and barracouta. Scallops, mussels and oysters are farmed both in the Nelson and Marlborough regions. The Kaikoura coast crayfish are unforgettable.

The South Island's west coast is famous for its whitebait available during spring. Fishing is one of the main industries of the West Coast, the albacore tuna being a very important export item to Japan. Menus of the area could also include flounders, sole, brill, turbot, hake and hoki.

Canterbury seas have different species, monkfish being one of the most unusual, red cod being popular. Around Timaru, south of Christchurch, elephant fish are a speciality.

In the deep south, rock lobster (crayfish) is the most valuable seafood catch. However, the Foveaux Strait or Bluff oysters are Southland's most famous delicacy. These make up but a few of the wide range of seafoods in New Zealand waters.

SPANISH SALAD WITH CRAYFISH :above

1 crayfish or lobster
1 medium onion
1 small green cucumber
1 green pepper (capsicum)
3 red tamarillos
salt and pepper

Caper dressing: ¼ cup mayonnaise
¼ cup sour cream
1 tablespoon capers
dash cayenne pepper

To prepare crayfish from the live state, immerse the fish in a large tub of cold water for about 2 hours. This will drown it. Place the crayfish in a saucepan of cold water and slowly bring to boiling point. Poach until the fish shell has turned red. Remove from the pan and cool. Refrigerate until required.

Using a heavy knife, cut the crayfish in half through the centre from the head to the tail. Clean head area by washing under the cold water tap. Drain. Scoop out the flesh and cut into cubes. Replace back into the shells. Dice onion and stand in icy water for 30 minutes. Drain. Dice pepper discarding seeds. Halve cucumber and scoop out seeds with a teaspoon. Cut cucumber into similar sized dice.

Peel 2 tamarillos and dice. Sprinkle with salt and pepper. Place diced pepper, tamarillo and cucumber into the top portion of the crayfish, keeping each vegetable separate. Place crayfish on a serving platter and surround with suitable green salad leaves. Placed diced onion on top. Cut remaining tamarillo in a zig-zag fashion through the centre, then pull apart. Place on platter for a garnish. Combine all ingredients for dressing. Serve separately.

Serves 2–3

FLOUNDER AND WHITEBAIT ROLLS WITH TAMARILLO SABAYON :right

Raw shrimp or crabmeat could be a substitute for the whitebait.

500 g (1 lb) flounder meat or fish suitable
  for rolling e.g. sole, dory
200 g (7 oz) small whitebait
25 g (1 oz) butter
salt and pepper

Tamarillo Sabayon: 3 tamarillos, peeled
2 tablespoons water
125 g (4 oz) clarified butter
1 egg yolk
salt and pepper
¼ cup cream

Lie fillets flat and top with equal amounts of whitebait. Dot with a little butter and sprinkle with salt and pepper. Roll up and secure with a small skewer. Place in a lightly buttered casserole and cover. This stage may be prepared well in advance—refrigerate until cooking time.

To prepare sabayon, slice tamarillos into a saucepan and add water. Cover and cook on low heat until soft. Purée then pass through a sieve. Melt the butter.

Place egg yolk in a blender or food processor and mix. Add tamarillo. With the motor running gradually pour in the butter. Season with salt and pepper and add cream. (This sauce may be kept warm in a vacuum flask.)

Cover and cook fish 180°C (350°F) for 20 minutes. Spoon a little sauce on a serving plate, carefully top with the fish roll and garnish with herbs.

OYSTERS AU NATURAL :above

New Zealand has two main species of oyster. Dredge oysters are available from April to August or until the quota has been filled. The main beds are in Foveaux Strait and some are found in Tasman Bay. The other main species is the Pacific oyster which is available on the half shell and as meat. It is farmed in the north of the North Island and will soon be farmed in Marlborough and Nelson.

6 to 12 oysters each on the half shell, per
  serving
1 slice of fresh wholemeal bread per
  serving
lemon juice
wedge of lemon for garnish

Arrange oysters each on their half shell on serving plate. Sprinkle with a little lemon juice. Serve with fingers of wholemeal bread. Garnish with lemon wedges.

8

Serves 4

The east coast of the Coromandel Peninsula near Hahei.

SMOKED EEL STARTER

250 g (9 oz) smoked eel
4 crisp lettuce leaves
½ babaco
crisp onion rings
sour cream
sprigs of dill

Thinly slice the smoked eel. Place lettuce leaves on 4 small serving plates. Arrange eel in the lettuce. Peel and slice babaco and place slices on the plate decoratively.

To crisp the onion rings, place sliced onion in icy water for 10 minutes. Just before serving scatter these over the eel. Pipe a little sour cream onto the plate and garnish with dill.

Serves 4

FANTASY FISH PLATE :above

Sauce: 1 cup tomato purée
finely grated rind and juice of 1 orange
½ teaspoon sugar
dash ground nutmeg

Timbales: 250 g (9 oz) skinned and boned
    white fish
2 tablespoons sour cream
1 egg, separated
salt and pepper
2 teaspoons horseradish
½ cup cream, whipped

8 mussels in shells
4 prawns or scampi, cooked
1 cleaned squid tube
5 thin slices smoked salmon

To prepare sauce, simmer purée, orange rind and juice, sugar and nutmeg for about 10 minutes for flavours to develop.

Meanwhile, to make timbales place fish in a food processor and purée.

Combine sour cream and egg yolk and cook over low heat until slightly thickened. Add to fish with seasonings. Beat egg white until stiff. Fold whipped cream and egg white into fish.

Place in 4 small well-greased ramekins and place in a baking pan containing hot water up to the level of the fish in the ramekins. Bake 30 minutes at 180°C (350°F).

Steam mussels until just opened. Warm prawns over the steam and pan-fry squid rings in a little oil about 1 minute until cooked.

Assemble two mussels, 1 prawn, 2–3 squid rings and some salmon on each serving plate. Spoon a little warm sauce on the plate and top with the fish timbale turned out of its mould.

Serves 4

The sun setting on Tahunanui Beach, Nelson.

HERBED ORANGE ROUGHY

500 g (1 lb) orange roughy
salt and freshly ground black pepper
sprigs of fresh rosemary and fennel

Divide fillets into 4 equal portions. Take 4 squares of lightly buttered foil or teflon coated foil and place fish in centre of each piece of foil. Sprinkle with seasonings and top with fresh herbs. Carefully wrap the fish. Seal well.

Place on a baking tray. Bake in the oven at 180°C (350°F) for about 15–20 minutes. Serve 1 packet per person.

Serves 4

SPINACH, SCALLOPS IN LIME COCONUT CREAM SAUCE :above

500 g (1 lb) spinach
500 g (1 lb) fresh scallops
1¼ cups fish stock
2 tablespoons clarified butter
½ onion, chopped
½ cup coconut cream
½ cup white wine
2 tablespoons sweet sherry
salt and pepper to taste
1 teaspoon chopped fresh coriander
   (cilantro)
juice and zest of 1 lime
2 tablespoons fresh cream
3–4 drops tabasco

Blanch the spinach in boiling salted water for 1 minute. Refresh under cold running water. Drain and squeeze out any excess moisture. Take a quarter of the spinach and purée in a blender with half of the fish stock.

Sauté the scallops in the very hot clarified butter, brown slightly, then remove from the pan and set aside in a warm place. Add a little more butter to the pan if necessary and sauté the onion.

Deglaze the pan with white wine, sherry and the remaining fish stock. Reduce by half. Add coconut cream, tabasco and lime juice, simmer for 2–3 minutes.

Meanwhile plunge remaining spinach into boiling water to heat through. Drain on paper towels, then lie onto warmed plates. Add the spinach purée and chopped coriander to the sauce. Taste for seasoning. Lastly add scallops to heat through, taking care not to overcook. Add the cream, divide scallops onto the prepared plates, pour over the sauce and serve. Sprinkle with a little zest of lime.

Serves 6

Rata in flower Totaranui, Abel Tasman National Park.

OVEN BAKED GREENSHELL MUSSELS
MARITIME :above

32 greenshell mussels
4 large tomatoes
1 clove garlic
100 g (3½ oz) artichoke bottoms
100 g (3½ oz) Mozzarella
1 sprig sage
1 tablespoon capers
1 cup crème fraîche
salt and freshly ground black pepper
2 egg yolks

Arrange mussels in gratin dishes. If they are frozen make sure they are just thawed and still icy. Peel and deseed tomatoes then roughly chop. Peel and finely chop garlic. Cut artichoke bottoms into fine wedges. Dice Mozzarella. Finely slice half of the sage.

Carefully mix the remaining ingredients. Spoon the mixture over the mussels. Bake at 180°C (350°F) for 10 minutes. Garnish with mussel shells and fresh sage leaves.

Serves 4

SOUTH SEAS KEBABS

2 minced paua (abalone)
250 g (9 oz) whole fish e.g. trevally, hoki,
    ling or warehou
1 cup soft breadcrumbs
1 small onion, finely chopped
1 egg
¾ cup wholemeal flour
salt and pepper
8 baby tomatoes
12 mushrooms

Mince or finely chop paua and fish together, then combine with breadcrumbs, onion and lightly beaten egg. Shape mixture into 16 small cakes, chill thoroughly or, if preferred, freeze for half an hour. Coat with seasoned wholemeal flour.

Bake uncovered in a well buttered ovenware dish at 200°C (400°F) for 10 minutes or shallow fry for 3–4 minutes on each side. Drain on absorbent paper. Thread fish cakes, tomato and mushroom onto 4 skewers. Warm under the grill before serving.

Serves 2–4

The active volcano of Mt Ngauruhoe, Tongariro
National Park.

POULTRY

Chickens have become popular fare during the last twenty years. This could be partly due to trends towards eating less red meat but is mainly because of the ready availability of chicken.

New Zealanders used to eat traditional roast chicken. However, it is now cooked in many ethnic ways as well as with local produce which makes it more "kiwi ethnic". The many new cuts and prepared portions have added interest to chicken recipes.

Turkey is a popular Christmas food but it is delicious in any seasonal menu. Small chickens, poussin, are now being farmed adding variety to the poultry scene.

TURKEY STRAWBERRY MINT SALAD :right

2.5 kg (5½ lb) turkey
50 g (2 oz) butter

Mint Dressing: ⅔ cup red currant jelly
¼ cup red wine vinegar
¼ cup oil
⅓ cup chopped fresh mint
salt and pepper

16 assorted lettuce leaves, washed and
    crisped
1 avocado, peeled and sliced
3 cups strawberries, sliced
extra mint leaves for garnish

Truss turkey, then brush with melted butter. Place in oven bag in a roasting dish and cook in oven at 160°C (325°F) for about 2–2½ hours. In a small saucepan, combine jelly, vinegar, oil, mint, salt and pepper. Heat until jelly is just melted.

Slice turkey and layer over a platter of assorted lettuce leaves. Top with avocado and strawberries. Pour warm dressing over just before serving. Garnish with extra mint leaves.

Serves 8

SPICED HONEY DRUMSTICKS :above

25 g (1 oz) butter, melted
1 teaspoon curry powder
¼ teaspoon salt
3 tablespoons German mustard or other
   mild prepared mustard
4 tablespoons honey
6 chicken drumsticks

Preheat oven to 180°C (350°F). Combine butter,
curry powder, salt, mustard and honey. Mix well. Coat
drumsticks in sauce. Place in a shallow baking dish.
Pour over remaining sauce. Bake for about 30 minutes
or until drumsticks are tender. Baste twice during
cooking time.

Place drumsticks on a serving dish. Spoon over sauce
to glaze or cool and chill in refrigerator before serving.

Serves 3–4

SMOKED CHICKEN SALAD

1 buttercrunch or red lettuce
1 smoked chicken
2 stalks celery
50 g (2 oz) unsalted nuts
1 spring onion, chopped

Dressing: 1 tablespoon lemon juice
3 tablespoons oil
½ teaspoon French mustard
salt and pepper
1 tablespoon sour cream

340 g (12 oz) can asparagus spears, drained

Separate lettuce leaves. Wash and drain. Cut chicken
into neat, finger-like pieces. Add celery, nuts and
spring onion.

Whisk ingredients for dressing until well combined.
Pour over chicken mixture and toss until mixed. Drain
asparagus spears. On a large platter arrange lettuce
leaves, asparagus and in the centre a stack of smoked
chicken.

Serves 4–6

The peaceful Whangaroa Harbour, Northland.

Kauri forest, Northland.

SMOKED CHICKEN PATE

200 g (7 oz) skinned and boned smoked
  chicken
1–2 tablespoons mayonnaise
2 teaspoons green/pink peppercorns (in
  brine)
1–2 teaspoons cracked peppercorns
a few red peppercorns if available

Place chicken in a food processor or through a
mincer until finely processed. Add enough mayonnaise
to make a thick paste. Wash green and/or red
peppercorns and combine with the chicken. Pack into
small pâté containers and sprinkle with cracked black
and red peppercorns. Serve with crusty bread.

Serves 6

TURKEY PROVENCE-STYLE :above

3.5 kg (8 lb) self-basting turkey
50 g (2 oz) butter, melted
3 rashers bacon, diced
I large carrot, peeled and diced
I large onion, peeled and diced
3 tablespoons brandy
salt and freshly ground black pepper
2 teaspoons paprika
I bunch fresh herbs e.g. sage, parsley,
    thyme
2 cloves garlic, crushed
200 g (7 oz) baby carrots
200 g (7 oz) button mushrooms
200 g (7 oz) tiny onions
3 tablespoons flour
25 g (I oz) butter (extra), softened
chopped parsley

Brush turkey with melted butter and place under a hot grill 1–2 minutes each side, until lightly golden.

Place the turkey in a large casserole. (Alternatively a roasting bag could be used.) Add the bottle of wine. Gently fry the bacon, diced carrot and onion in remaining butter until lightly coloured. Add brandy and flame. Add to casserole. Season then add paprika, herbs and garlic. Cover casserole tightly and cook at 160°C (325°F) for 1 hour.

Meanwhile steam baby carrots and onions. Add with mushrooms to casserole after the 1 hour and continue cooking for another 40–50 minutes.

Cream flour and softened butter until smooth then whisk small knobs into the casserole juices to thicken. Sprinkle with chopped parsley before serving.

Serves 8–10

21

MEXICAN CHICKEN WITH KIWIFRUIT AND PAWPAW SALSA :above

1 large egg
3 tablespoons Mexican (chilli) tomato sauce
1 cup dry breadcrumbs
½ teaspoon each chilli powder, ground
   cumin, oregano
3 whole chicken breasts, skinned, boned
   and halved
25 g (1 oz) butter
2 tablespoons oil

Salsa: 3 kiwifruit
½ small pawpaw (papaya)
2 tablespoons chopped coriander (cilantro)
2 shallots, diced

Beat egg with Mexican tomato sauce. Combine breadcrumbs with seasonings. Dip chicken halves in egg mixture then in breadcrumbs pressing in well. Refrigerate to set coating about 30 minutes.

Melt butter and oil in a roasting pan. Add chicken, turn to coat in butter and oil. Bake at 180°C (350°F) for about 25 minutes or until cooked.

Meanwhile peel and dice kiwifruit and pawpaw. Place in a bowl with coriander and shallots. Serve with the chicken.

Serves 6

Sheep yards in winter, South Island Mackenzie Country.

GRILLED CHICKEN FILLETS WITH APRICOT SAUCE

4 boneless chicken breast fillets
25 g (1 oz) butter, melted
4 rashers bacon

Sauce: 75 g (3 oz) chopped dried apricots
½ cup water
1 tablespoon butter
1 clove garlic, crushed
½ small onion, finely chopped
½–1 cup water
2 teaspoons sugar
1 tablespoon wine vinegar
2 tablespoons pinenuts

Remove skin from chicken. Brush fillets with melted butter. Wrap a bacon rasher around each fillet. Place on lightly greased grill tray. Grill for about 10 minutes, turning once during cooking.

To prepare sauce, place apricots and ½ cup water in a medium sized pan. Cover, bring to the boil then simmer for 5–7 minutes or until apricots are soft. Mash to a purée. In a small pan, melt butter. Add garlic and onion. Cook gently for 2 minutes or until softened.

To apricots, add onion mixture, 1 cup water, vinegar and sugar. Simmer uncovered for 5 minutes or until sauce has thickened. Mix in pinenuts. Serve chicken fillets with apricot sauce.

Serves 4

Coopers Beach, Northland.

NEW ZEALAND MEAT

The New Zealand meat industry has been the backbone of our existence for over 100 years. Our lamb is enjoyed in many countries around the world where it is cooked in a multiplicity of ways. Once the common method of preparing lamb was roasting it in the English style. However, nowadays lamb is minced, diced, made into steaks, barbecued, microwaved, stir-fried, and cooked in many international recipes.

Beef dishes too have undergone change. Roasts and boiling cuts are less popular than they were. Today's emphasis is on quick cooking steaks, kebabs, minced meats and hamburgers that fit the lifestyle of most New Zealanders.

The country is famous for its "3 million people and 70 million sheep". The largest sheep population is centred around the Canterbury region, followed by the Wairarapa and Manawatu areas and the South Auckland, Bay of Plenty and Hawkes Bay regions.

Most beef cattle are raised in conjunction with sheep and enjoy year round outside pasture which results in good flesh taste and texture. There are about 5 million cattle in New Zealand.

Pork and its variations are enjoyed by many. Glazed hams are popular at Christmas providing cool cuts for warmer days.

OUTDOOR PORK :above

6 chops or steaks (preferably cut from the
  forequarter)
¼ cup dry sherry
½ cup tomato purée
1 teaspoon ground ginger
1 small onion, grated
1 teaspoon mustard
2 tablespoons honey
1 tablespoon Worcestershire sauce
2 tablespoons oil

Snip edges of chops and place in single layer in a flat
pan. Combine all other ingredients well. Pour over
pork and marinate for at least 4 hours. Drain excess
marinade from meat and barbecue over hot coals for
about 12–15 minutes each side or until cooked as
desired.

Serves 6

BEEF, BACON AND OYSTER CASSEROLE

750 g (1½ lb) stewing steak
2 rashers bacon
1 bay leaf
1 sprig parsley
1 large onion, chopped
1 large carrot, chopped
100 g (3½ oz) mushrooms, sliced
salt
freshly ground black pepper
3 tablespoons flour
1 tablespoon oil
1 tablespoon butter
1 cup red wine or stock
12 large oysters
small bacon rolls for garnish (optional)

Cut meat into 3 cm (1¼") cubes. Dice bacon. Combine meats with bay leaf, parsley, onion, carrot and mushrooms. Sprinkle with salt, pepper and flour and mix well.

Heat oil and butter in a wide pan. Sauté mixture in batches until slightly browned. Turn into a casserole dish. Pour in wine. Cover and cook at 160°C (325°F) for 2 hours. Add oysters and any oyster liquid. Bake a further 30 minutes.

Garnish with small rolls of bacon which have been grilled. Serve with baked potatoes and a crisp salad.

Serves 5

LAMB NOISETTES JOHN :right

1.25 kg (3 lb) boned and rolled loin of lamb,
   tied with string every 4 cm (1¼")
salt and pepper
4 cloves garlic
1–2 tablespoons dried tarragon
oil
¼ cup brandy
¾ cup cream
½ cup red currants (in season) or use jelly

Rub lamb with salt and pepper. Crush garlic and pound with tarragon. Spread lamb with this mixture and pan fry or roast. To pan fry, cut steaks in middle between each string, leaving 1 string per steak. Heat 2 tablespoons oil in heavy frypan and fry noisettes on medium heat, 10 minutes each side. Transfer to hot platter and keep warm.

To roast, place in roasting dish and brush with a little oil. Roast at 180°C (350°F) for about 45 minutes. Place lamb on warm platter and cut into noisettes. Retain pan juices, add brandy and cream. Bring to boil and simmer for a few minutes, stirring constantly. Add red currants or jelly, heat through and pour over noisettes.

Serves 6–8

Queenstown, Lake Wakatipu and the Remarkables in
the grips of winter.

LAMBURGERS :above

750 g (1½ lb) lean minced lamb
¼ cup dry breadcrumbs
1 egg, beaten
1½ teaspoons ground coriander
grated rind and juice of ½ orange
2 tablespoons soy sauce
2 tablespoons oil
6 hamburger buns

Garnishes: lettuce, mayonnaise, tomato
   slices, onion rings, cucumber or orange
   slices, olives, parsley

Combine lamb, breadcrumbs, egg, coriander, rind and juice of orange and soy sauce. Divide mixture into 6 equal parts and shape into patties. Heat oil in frypan and sauté patties about 4 minutes each side.

Meanwhile heat 6 hamburger buns. Halve and butter thinly. Place layers of lettuce and mayonnaise on the base and 2 tomato slices. Top with meat patties, onion rings and slices of cucumber or orange. Place other half buns on top and garnish with olive and parsley secured by toothpicks.

Serves 6

28

Pastoral scene Leslie Hills station, North Canterbury.

TRADITIONAL BEEF CASSEROLE

500 g (1 lb) stewing steak, cubed
¼ cup seasoned flour
1 tablespoon oil
1 leek, sliced
2 stalks celery, sliced
1 carrot, sliced
½ cup beer
¾ cup beef stock

Topping: 1 cup flour
3 tablespoons dried milk powder
2 teaspoons baking powder
1 tablespoon butter
1 cup shredded Cheddar cheese
5–6 tablespoons water

Toss meat in seasoned flour to coat well, then sauté in hot oil until lightly browned. Add leek, celery and carrot and cook for 1–2 minutes. Pour in beer and stock, bring to the boil and then pour into a medium casserole. Cover and cook at 180°C (350°F) for 1½–2 hours or until tender.

To prepare the topping, sift flour, milk powder and baking powder into a bowl and rub in butter. Stir in half the cheese and add sufficient water to make a soft dough. Pat out to about 1 cm (½") thick and cut into triangles. Place on the hot stew. Sprinkle with remaining cheese. Bake at 200°C (400°F) for 12–15 minutes.

Serves 4

SPICY PORK SPARERIBS :above

1 kg (2 lb) pork spareribs
2 cloves garlic
1 teaspoon salt
black pepper
½ teaspoon five spice powder
1 tablespoon honey
1 tablespoon oil
3 tablespoons light soy sauce

Leave the spareribs as long strips. Place on a lightly greased grill tray. Crush the garlic to a paste with the salt and combine with the remaining ingredients. Brush the mixture thickly onto both sides of the ribs. Reserve the remaining mixture.

Grill spareribs 30–35 minutes. Brush with any remaining mixture during cooking. Cut between each rib before serving.

30   Serves 4

GLAZED LEG OF LAMB WITH
TAMARILLO SAUCE :above

1 carvery or whole leg of lamb
2 cloves garlic, slivered
¼ cup red currant jelly
½ teaspoon dried marjoram
1 teaspoon finely grated orange rind
2 tablespoons orange juice

Sauce: 500 g (1 lb) tamarillos
1 small onion, chopped
¼–½ cup red currant jelly
¼ cup marsala wine (optional)

Using a sharp knife, make slits in lamb and insert slivers of garlic. Place lamb in roasting pan. Cook at 180°C (350°F) for 20–25 minutes per 500 g (1 lb). Turn halfway through cooking time and brush with glaze. Fifteen minutes before the end of cooking time, brush with remaining glaze and leave right side up for completion of cooking.

To prepare glaze, whisk together jelly, marjoram, orange rind and juice.

To prepare sauce—cover tamarillos with boiling water, then immerse in cold water. Remove skins. Roughly chop tamarillos and purée in food processor or blender with the onion and jelly. Transfer sauce to a small saucepan. Stir in the marsala and simmer gently 3–4 minutes. Strain if desired. Serve lamb hot or cold with tamarillo sauce, and vegetables or salad.

Serve 6

Koputauaki Bay and pohutukawa tree, Coromandel
Peninsula's west coast.

ROLLED LAMB AND SPINACH :above

150 g (5 oz) pumpkin, peeled and cut into 2
    cm (¾") cubes
100 g (3½ oz) cream cheese
2 tablespoons pinenuts
1 tablespoon dried breadcrumbs
½ teaspoon dried oregano
salt and pepper
2 tablespoons beaten egg
4 lamb schnitzels
4 spinach leaves

Steam pumpkin until tender. Mash together
pumpkin and cream cheese. Mix in the pinenuts,
breadcrumbs, seasonings and egg. Refrigerate 10
minutes.

Place schnitzels on a flat board. Place a washed
drained spinach leaf on each. Spread a portion of
filling over the spinach. Roll up schnitzels, tucking in
spinach if necessary and secure with toothpicks.

Place rolls on grill tray. Grill for 12 minutes and turn
halfway through the cooking time. Cool rolls, remove
toothpicks, then wrap in plastic film and refrigerate
–12 hours. Cut into slices to serve.

Serves 4–6

RIBBON PORK WITH BUTTER AND CUMIN

*Quick cooking, the pork fillet is cut into thin strips then
threaded onto skewers in a ribbon-like way.*

1 kg (2 lb) pork fillet
50 g (2 oz) butter
2 cloves garlic, crushed
2 teaspoons ground cumin

Pre-soak about 16 bamboo skewers in cold water
about 15 minutes. Cut pork fillet in thin ribbons about
1 cm (½") wide and 5 mm (¼") thick. Thread in a
ribbon-like way onto skewers. Place in a shallow dish.
Melt butter and add garlic and cumin. Brush the pork
ribbons well. Allow to stand about 2 hours at room
temperature, brushing again after 1 hour.

Grill over high heat about 1 minute each side. Serve
with soy sauce as a dipping sauce.

Serves 5–6

33

Lake Tekapo, a high country lake in the South Island,
and the Richmond Range.

GAME AND GAMEFISH

Deer were first introduced to the central North
Island and the South Island about 1851. After erosion
became a problem due to the deer eating and destroying
vegetation, organised deerstalker associations were set up
to organise hunting. Deer farming began in the mid-1960s
and venison is growing into a major export industry.
Venison is readily available on restaurant menus and is
becoming more so for home cooks.

Many game birds are now being farmed especially
in the Taranaki area. Duck, geese, quails, guinea fowl and
different breeds of duck are available and like farmed
venison, the flesh of the birds has a mild flavour
compared to the wild equivalents.

Salmon were introduced to South Island rivers in
the 1870s and New Zealand is thought to be the only
place where salmon have survived outside their native
habitat of North America. Catching salmon is a luxury but
happily salmon farming has let us enjoy this delicate fish
more easily. Trout are not farmed as yet but can be caught
in Lake Taupo and its rivers, Lake Rotorua, as well as
many other small North Island lakes.

CAMP-FIRE TROUT :above

1 kg (2 lb) prepared trout
butter
salt and pepper
fresh thyme, optional

Remove head and tail from trout. Split open and lie flat. Brush with butter and season.

Place skin-side down preferably in a wire fish grill. Cook over glowing coals for about 5–7 minutes, brushing once or twice with more butter. Remove skin before eating.

Serves about 4

MARINATED FRESH SALMON

A delicious starter.

½ cup lemon juice
1 small onion, chopped
dash Tabasco
1 teaspoon sugar
½ teaspoon white pepper
500 g (1 lb) fresh salmon
shredded lettuce
parsley sprigs
lemon twists

Combine juice, onion, and seasonings. Discard any bones and skin from salmon and cut flesh into small dice. Add to the marinade and refrigerate for 6–8 hours, until the fish takes on a cooked appearance. Drain.

Serve on lettuce garnished with parsley and lemon.

Serves 6

SALMON STEAKS WITH HOLLANDAISE SAUCE :above

Hollandaise sauce: 100 g (3½ oz) butter
2 large egg yolks
1 tablespoon lemon juice
1 tablespoon white wine vinegar
white pepper
2 teaspoons boiling water

Salmon: 4 salmon steaks, about 500 g (1 lb)
4 tablespoons chopped fresh herbs
25 g (1 oz) butter
juice 1 lemon
fresh herbs for garnish

To prepare sauce melt butter over low heat.

Combine egg yolks, lemon juice and vinegar in a bowl then whisk in melted butter. Cook in double boiler, stirring once or twice until sauce just begins to thicken. Season with salt and pepper then add boiling water. This sauce may be kept warm in a vacuum flask for two hours before being served.

To cook fish, place in a large greased frypan. Dot with herbs and butter. Cover and cook for 5 minutes on low heat. Stand 2 minutes then sprinkle with lemon juice. Place on serving plates and garnish with fresh herbs. Serve with Hollandaise sauce.

Serves 4

Bay, Lake Wanaka.

Sunrise over Tongariro National Park from Hikumutu.

TROUT AND KIWI VINAIGRETTE :above

750 g (1½ lb) trout
2 large kiwifruit
3 tablespoons olive oil
1 tablespoon white wine vinegar
salt and freshly ground black pepper
fresh dill for garnishing

Discard the head from the trout, trim tails and fins and clean. Wrap loosely in oiled foil. Place in a roasting dish and bake at 150°C (300°F) for about 30 minutes. Unwrap and allow to cool before carefully removing the skin—boning is optional.

Meanwhile peel and slice the kiwifruit. Purée and sieve one kiwifruit. Whisk the pulp with the oil and vinegar. Season well. Garnish the trout with the remaining kiwifruit and dill. Serve the dressing separately.

Serves 2

TROUT WITH WILD RICE AND ORANGE

750 g (1½ lb) trout
¾ cup wild rice
3 cups boiling water
1 teaspoon salt
grated rind 1 orange
1 teaspoon finely grated root ginger
2 tablespoons chopped chives or dill

Garnish: sprig dill
segments of 1 orange

Clean the trout trimming tail and fins if necessary. Wash rice well. If required, half long grain white rice and half wild rice could be used.

Bring water to the boil, add salt and rice. Simmer for about 35 minutes or until cooked. Drain well.

Add orange rind, ginger and chives. Spoon into the centre of the trout. Place in a greased baking pan and cover with foil. Bake at 150°C (300°F) for about 30–40 minutes until cooked. Serve garnished with dill and orange segments.

Serves 4–5

Toi Tois and Kaimanawa Mountains, central North Island.

ROAST WILD DUCK OR GOOSE

    I duck or goose
    I small onion
    2 stalks celery
    sprig fresh thyme
    salt and freshly ground black pepper
    I large onion, diced
    2 carrots, diced
    2 tablespoons butter
    I rasher bacon
    I cup water

Fill cavity with sliced onion, celery and thyme. Sprinkle bird with salt and pepper. Tie or truss. Sauté diced onion and carrots in butter until just soft. Transfer to a baking dish just large enough to hold the bird.

Place bird on vegetables. Top with bacon and add water. Cover with foil and bake 180°C (350°F) for 25 minutes per 500 g (1 lb) or until tender. Remove foil for the last half hour of cooking. Prick the skin to allow excess fat to escape. Serve with gravy made from pan juices, a tart jelly and baked kumara.

40 Serves 2–3 for duck or 4–6 for goose

OVEN BAKED QUAIL WITH HERB SAUCE :right

    8 quail
    75 g (3 oz) butter, melted
    I teaspoon coffee powder
    ¼ cup wholemeal flour
    salt and pepper

    Herb Sauce: 425 g (15 oz) can savoury
        tomatoes
    2 tablespoons red wine
    ¼ cup finely chopped fresh herbs, e.g.
        parsley with basil or rosemary
    fresh herbs for garnish

Brush quail with melted butter combined with the coffee powder. Place flour and seasonings in a paper or plastic bag and shake quail in flour to coat. Brush a large roasting pan with butter mixture, add quail and brush lightly with remaining butter. Bake at 200°C (400°F) for about 15 minutes until cooked.

Meanwhile simmer lightly mashed tomatoes, wine and herbs for 10 minutes in a saucepan. Spoon sauce on a serving plate and top with quail. Garnish with fresh herbs.

Serves 4

Godley Peak (centre left) and Lake Tekapo.

VENISON WITH TART CHERRY SAUCE :left

750 g (1½ lb) hind steak (grilling) venison
2 tablespoons smooth mustard
1 tablespoon each chopped rosemary and
  parsley
1 tablespoon mustard seeds
Cherry Sauce: 1 cup red wine
¼ cup lemon juice
1–2 tablespoons golden (or maple) syrup
1 tablespoon cornflour (cornstarch)
¼ cup water
salt and pepper
finely grated rind of 1 lemon
2 cups cherries, fresh, frozen or preserved

Place venison on a rack folding thinner parts under, and spread top with 1 tablespoon mustard. Place under a pre-heated medium-hot grill for about 6 minutes.

Turn meat over and spread with remaining mustard, herbs and mustard seeds and continue cooking for 6–8 minutes. May be served warmed or chilled.

To make sauce combine wine, lemon juice, golden syrup and cornflour mixed with water. Heat, stirring until thick. Taste for seasonings. Add peel, salt and pepper. Add cherries reserving a few for garnish. Serve warm or at room temperature with thinly sliced venison.

Serves 8

FABULOUS 5 MINUTE VENISON

500 g (1 lb) venison hind steak
1 tablespoon olive oil
1 tablespoon finely grated root ginger
2 green peppers (capsicum)
1 clove garlic, crushed
freshly ground black pepper
3 tablespoons red wine
2 medium tomatoes, quartered

Cut meat 5 mm (¼") thick, in 2.5 cm (1") squares.

Heat a heavy frypan over high heat. Add oil, swirling around the sides then the ginger and venison, stirring well. Add peppers, garlic and black pepper, stirring constantly. Pour in wine and continue stir-frying for about 2 minutes. Add tomatoes and cook 1 minute to heat through. Serve immediately with rice or noodles.

Serves 4

Falls Creek on the road from Te Anau to Milford,
Fiordland National Park.

VEGETABLES

The temperate climate and fertile soils of New Zealand provide the ideal conditions for luxurious growth of an incredible range of vegetables. Leafy greens, squash and pumpkins, pods and seeds, tubers and root vegetables thrive in soils throughout the country.

Many vegetables from New Zealand are found in world markets. September's asparagus from Hawkes Bay is air freighted around the world. Onions are exported to Japan along with squash and pumpkin.

The kumara (sweet potato) could be called indigenous to this country. A favourite food throughout Polynesia, the Maori developed great skill in cultivating this tasty tuber. It has developed into a larger vegetable from the original and has a special place in kiwi cuisine.

At Pukekohe, south of Auckland, are huge market gardens based on volcanic soils. These supply the largest city with fresh vegetables. In the centre of the North Island near the base of Mt Ruapehu, Ohakune has gained a reputation for its Brussels sprouts, carrots and parsnips. Manawatu and Marlborough grow most of the country's shallots and garlic. Swede is the signature vegetable of Southland, while potatoes and Brussels sprouts are plentiful in the Timaru/Oamaru area.

Throughout the country, herb gardening is becoming fashionable helping to complement the produce of the land.

VEGETABLE SEAFOOD SALAD :above

Parsley Dressing: ¼ cup chopped parsley
2 tablespoons capers
2 tablespoons white vinegar
1 tablespoon chopped chives
½ cup mayonnaise

Salad: 750 g (1½ lb) medium textured,
    skinless, boneless fish fillets
2 tablespoons lemon juice
8 large lettuce leaves
2 tomatoes, cut in wedges
½ cucumber, sliced
100 g (3½ oz) mushrooms, halved
2 medium carrots, peeled and cut in thin
    strips
100 g (3½ oz) green beans, cut lengthwise
    and lightly blanched
½ cup French dressing

To make parsley dressing: combine parsley, capers, vinegar and chives in a food processor and process until smooth. Fold parsley mixture into the mayonnaise and mix well. Cover and chill 1 hour.

Brush fish fillets with lemon juice. Foil bake, steam or microwave fillets until they just flake when tested with a fork. Allow fish to cool a little then cut into 1.5 cm (½") cubes.

Line a large serving platter with lettuce leaves. Coat fish with parsley dressing and pile into the centre of the platter. Toss the individual lots of prepared vegetables in French dressing and arrange in groups around the fish. Chill until ready to serve. Serve with French bread.

Serves 4

45

Looking down Dusky Sound, Fiordland National Park.

CHILLED CUCUMBER SOUP

30 cm (12") cucumber
2 medium tomatoes
1 green or red pepper (capsicum)
1 cup plain sweetened low fat yoghurt
3 sprigs mint
freshly ground black pepper

Garnish: sprigs fresh mint, cucumber slices

Peel the cucumber, cut lengthwise and remove the seeds. Purée the cucumber, tomatoes, pepper, yoghurt and fresh mint until finely blended. Season with freshly ground black pepper. Serve chilled. Garnish with fresh mint and cucumber slices.

Serves 4–5

YAM KEBABS WITH SOY AND GINGER GLAZE :above

24 yams
2 leeks
3 cm (1") knob root ginger
1 red or green pepper (capsicum)

Glaze: ½ cup soy sauce
½ cup Mirin or sweet rice wine
1–2 tablespoons sugar
trimmings from the ginger
½ teaspoon ground cumin
1 teaspoon ground coriander

Scrub and trim the yams. Cook in boiling salted water for 15 minutes until just done. Cut leeks into 3 cm (1") lengths and lightly blanch. Cut red or green pepper into rectangles roughly the size of the yams and leek slices. Slice the ginger 5 mm (¼") thick.

Thread onto bamboo skewers, firstly a piece of pepper, then a yam, a slice of ginger, a piece of leek and so on.

Place all the ingredients for the glaze into a saucepan and boil for 5 minutes. Strain to remove the ginger root. Sauté the yam kebabs, brown slightly on both sides, then pour in a little of the glaze. Baste constantly until the vegetables are complete cooked and glazed.

Transfer to a warmed serving platter and pour the remaining glaze over the kebabs then serve.

Serves 4

47

Springtime at Blandford Lodge Stud, Waikato.

AVOCADO BLT

half a ripe avocado
small lettuce leaves
1 sesame seed roll
1 rasher bacon, grilled
1 tomato sliced
salt and freshly ground black pepper

Peel avocado, slice and fan out. Halve the bun and top with lettuce leaves, avocado, bacon and tomato. Season with salt and pepper.

Serves 1

PUMPKIN PASTA :above

500 g (1 lb) peeled pumpkin
1 large onion
½ cup water
3 bay leaves
freshly ground black pepper
¼ teaspoon ground nutmeg
½ cup light sour cream
6 slices salami
¼ cup pumpkin seeds
1 teaspoon margarine
325 g (11 oz) dried pasta or 500 g (1 lb)
   fresh pasta

Roughly chop the pumpkin and onion. Place the pumpkin, onion, water and bay leaves in a saucepan of salted water. Cover and cook until the pumpkin is tender. Remove the bay leaves. Purée with the pepper, nutmeg and sour cream. Finely chop the salami.

Place the pumpkin seeds and margarine in a shallow pan, cover and cook gently until just changing colour. Cook the pasta according to the instructions on the packet. Drain. Place on serving dishes, pour over the hot pumpkin sauce, sprinkle with the salami and pumpkin seeds.

Parmesan cheese or grated cheddar cheese is also good sprinkled over the top.

Serves 4–6

49

HOT GREEN SALAD WITH HONEY HERB DRESSING :above

6 cups assorted green vegetables, e.g.
  broccoli flowerets
  finely sliced courgettes (zucchini)
  sliced celery
  chopped green pepper (capsicum)
  bean sprouts
  halved Brussels sprouts
  finely sliced cabbage
  Chinese cabbage
  spinach

Honey Herb Dressing:
  2 tablespoons honey
  2 tablespoons spiced vinegar
  1 tablespoon oil
  2 tablespoons finely chopped fresh herbs

Place prepared vegetables in a saucepan of boiling salted water, cover and cook until just tender but still slightly crisp—about 1–2 minutes. If using green leafy vegetables such as cabbage or spinach, add after 1 minute. Drain well. Pour hot dressing over vegetables and serve immediately.

Serves 6

VEGETABLES WITH NAVARIN OR GREENSHELL MUSSELS :above

32 mussels in the half shell
3 cups fish stock
16 baby carrots, trimmed and cleaned
16 baby turnips, trimmed and cleaned
100 g (3½ oz) broccoli flowerets
100 g (3½ oz) each red and green peppers
   (capsicum), cut in 3 cm (1") squares
16 button mushrooms
8 cherry tomatoes

Sauce: ½ cup stock
juice of 2 limes
250 g (9 oz) butter, diced
1 tablespoon fresh parsley
1 tablespoon fresh basil
ground pepper
Garnish: fresh coriander

Bring fish stock to the boil in a pot with a tight fitting lid. Add the turnips and carrots, cover and cook for 2 minutes. Add mussels, peppers, broccoli and mushrooms. Replace lid and steam 2–3 minutes. Remove lid, add cherry tomatoes. Remove half cup of mussel/fish stock, add the lime juice, reduce a little, then whisk in the butter to make a beurre blanc-style sauce. Add the parsley, basil and pepper.

Lift the mussels and vegetables from the stock, arrange on the plates and coat with the sauce.

Serves 4

KUMARA AND PUMPKIN :above

    1 medium kumara, scrubbed
    325 g (11 oz) pumpkin, peeled
    1 tablespoon oil
    2 rashers lean bacon, finely chopped
    1 clove garlic, peeled and finely chopped

Boil the kumara and pumpkin until tender but still firm. Cut into bite-sized chunks. Heat the oil in a large pan or wok. Add the bacon and garlic and sauté for 2–3 minutes. Add the pumpkin and kumara and stir-fry for 4–5 minutes or until the vegetables are cooked. Serve immediately.

Serves 4

52

Traditional Maori cooking in the hot pools at
Whakarewarewa village, Rotorua.

ELSBERG POTATO SKINS

4 medium potatoes, baked
1 cup bacon, cooked and crumbled
250 g/9oz Elsberg cheese, grated
1 egg, lightly beaten
2 tablespoons chopped green chillies
2 tablespoons pimento (red pepper),
   optional
2 spring onions, diced
sour cream
chopped chives

Cut potatoes in half lengthwise. Scoop out all but 5
mm (¼") of pulp. Combine bacon, 1½ cups cheese, egg,
chillies, pimento and onion, blending well. Spread
evenly in potato shells. Sprinkle with remaining cheese.

Bake in preheated oven 180°C (350°F) for 15–20
minutes or until cheese is melted and bubbly. Serve
with sour cream and chives if desired. Cut each in half
to serve as snacks.

Serves 8 as a main course accompaniment or 16 snacks

53

Autumn Lakes Hayes, Central Otago.

PUMPKIN SOUP:right

> 500 g (I lb) peeled and seeded pumpkin
> 2 tablespoons butter
> 2 onions, sliced
> 4 cups chicken stock
> ½ teaspoon salt
> I stalk celery, chopped
> I large potato, peeled and chopped
> I tablespoon lemon juice
> ¼ teaspoon Tabasco sauce
> I teaspoon paprika
> ¼–½ cup whipping cream

Cut pumpkin in cubes and chop in food processor to get a coarse pulp. Heat butter in a saucepan. Add onions and pumpkin and cook stirring occasionally for 5 minutes. Gradually stir in the stock, salt, celery, potato, lemon juice, Tabasco and paprika and bring to the boil.

Reduce the heat to low, cover and simmer for about 20 minutes or until the pumpkin and vegetables are tender.

Place in a food processor and process to get a smooth purée. Stir in the cream and return to the saucepan. Heat stirring constantly for a few minutes or until the soup is very hot but not boiling.

STEAMED ASPARAGUS WITH TANGY LEMON SAUCE

> 100 ml (3½ fl oz) lemon juice
> 2 tablespoons wine
> grated rind of I lemon
> I tablespoon butter
> 2 egg yolks
> 2 tablespoons cream or sour cream
> 500 g (I lb) prepared asparagus

To make sauce, bring lemon juice, wine, rind and butter to the boil. Whisk in egg yolks and cook until thick. Stir in cream.

Meanwhile steam or boil asparagus until just tender. Serve with the lemon sauce.

54   Serves 4–5

Serves 6

Champagne Pool, Waiotapu thermal region, Rotorua.

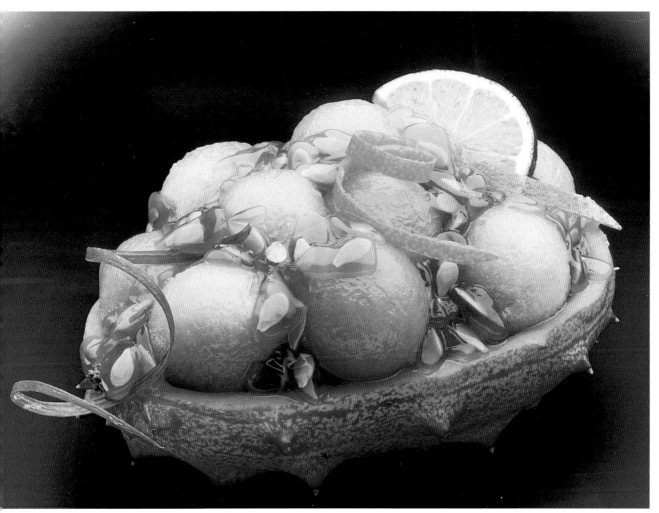

FRUIT

This country has built a world-wide reputation for the development of new fruits. The kiwifruit, previously named the Chinese gooseberry, has made New Zealand famous in the horticulture scene. The original fruit was small, round and very fuzzy with a very different flavour. Today's kiwifruit is almost bald, it is oval and has a refreshing tang.

Unusual fruits being exported are tamarillos, pepinos, persimmons, nashi, feijoas, passionfruit and kiwanos. Many originated from South America but often these have been improved upon by local horticulturalists.

The north of the North Island grows wonderful citrus—navel oranges, lemons, grapefruit, mandarins and tangelos. Because the area is sub-tropical it also produces tamarillos, kiwifruit and feijoas in abundance.

The colder areas in winter are generally the apple and pear growing districts. Hawkes Bay, Nelson and Central Otago also grow nashi, the Asian pear. Top quality stone fruit and berries are another feature of Hawkes Bay and Central Otago. The Bay of Plenty region is really the hub of the kiwifruit industry but also grows citrus, tamarillos and the other unusual sub-tropicals.

The recipes in this chapter are for more savoury dishes or preserves. Other fruit recipes may be sourced in the dessert section.

KIWANO AND MARINATED MELON :above

2 kiwano
½ large rock melon (canteloupe)
½ large honeydew melon
1½ tablespoons orange liqueur
1 tablespoon sugar

Garnish: strips of orange rind
and strips of lemon rind

Cut kiwano in half lengthwise and, using a fork, scoop out pulp into bowl. Reserve shells for serving. Remove seeds from melons and using a melon baller, scoop melon out to make balls. Place melon balls into bowl, add liqueur and sugar and let stand 20 minutes.

At serving time, arrange melon balls in kiwano shells and spoon kiwano pulp onto melon. Garnish with orange and lemon.

Serves 4 as fruit starter or dessert

CITRUS SALAD :above

4 oranges, peeled and sliced
1 cup sprouts (e.g. mung, aduki, lentil,
    radish, pea or a mixed pack)
2 spring onions, finely sliced
2 tablespoons spiced vinegar
1 tablespoon oil
freshly ground black pepper
1 teaspoon sugar

Mix the orange slices, spouts and spring onions together in a bowl. Blend the vinegar, oil, pepper and sugar together. Pour over the orange slice mixture. Chill.

Serves 4–6

Mountaineers on the Fox Glacier, Southern Alps.

TAMARILLO SAUCE

This simple sauce is delicious. Prepare in bulk and store in refrigerator for up to one week or in deep freeze for up to one year. Use as a base for drinks or as a topping for ice cream.

> 500 g (1 lb) tamarillos
> ¼ cup sugar

Pour boiling water over tamarillos in a bowl and stand 2 minutes. Drain and cover in cold water. Peel. Slice into the bowl of the food processor. Sprinkle with sugar (add more sugar if preferred). Stand for 30 minutes for juices to develop. Purée using the metal blade. Pour into a jug to serve.

Serves 4–6

Kiwifruit orchards beside Tauranga Harbour.

NASHI WITH BLACKBERRY CREAM

Serve as a starter or as an ending to dinner.

> 2 cups blackberries
> 2 tablespoons crème fraîche (or sour
>   cream)
> 2 nashi
> lemon juice
> 25 g (1 oz) butter
> 1 teaspoon ground coriander

Purée the blackberries and cream and sieve. Sweeten or add lemon juice as desired. Cut nashi across in 5 mm (¼") slices leaving cores intact. Sprinkle with lemon juice to prevent browning.

Melt butter in a large shallow frypan. Pan-fry slices in a single layer about 30 seconds each side.

Place two slices on each serving plate and spoon a little of the sauce alongside. Sprinkle nashi with a little coriander. Can be garnished with extra berries if required.

Serves about 6

KIWANO SMOOTHIE :above

> pulp of 1 kiwano
> 1 cup plain yoghurt
> 1 tablespoon honey
> 2 scoops vanilla ice cream

Place all ingredients in a blender or food processor and blend until smooth.

Serve in long glasses or in kiwanos which have had one end removed and have been hollowed out.

Serves 1–2

Dairy herd and the Kaikoura Range.

PLUM SOUP

1 kg (2 lb) can or jar preserved dark plums,
    chilled
2 tablespoons sugar
2 tablespoons lemon juice
⅛ teaspoon each ground cinnamon,
    nutmeg, cloves
whipped cream

Drain fruit, remove any stones, and purée. Add
enough liquid to make a medium-thin soup. Blend in
sugar, lemon juice and seasonings. Serve garnished
with cream.

Serves 4–6

PEPINO, PROSCUITTO WITH MUSTARD
AND HAZELNUT OIL VINAIGRETTE :above

2 pepino
8 slices prosciutto
salad greens

Vinaigrette: 1 tablespoon French mustard
zest and juice of 1 lime
juice of 1 lemon
¾ cup hazelnut oil
2 tablespoons chopped chervil
salt and pepper to taste

Arrange sliced pepino and proscuitto attractively on
a plate with salad greens. Combine vinaigrette
ingredients and dress the salad.

Serves 4   63

Hill pattern of tussock and snow Lindis Pass, Otago.

PERSIMMON AND ORANGE SALAD :right

2 non-astringent persimmon (kaki), sliced
2 oranges, peeled and sliced
grapes, almonds and kiwifruit for garnish

Layer slices of persimmon and orange onto a serving platter. Scatter with grapes, almonds and kiwifruit. Serve with yoghurt dressing as a starter or with lightly whipped cream as a dessert.

Serves 4–6

LEMON HONEY

4 lemons
4 eggs
2 cups sugar
125 g (4 oz) butter

Grate rind of lemons and squeeze out juice. Beat eggs lightly. Place all ingredients into top part of double boiler and cook over boiling water, stirring until thick.

Pour into hot jars and seal with vacuum seals or preserving wax. May be stored in refrigerator for several weeks if unsealed. Mandarin, orange or grapefruit honey can be made in the same way.

Makes about 2 cups.

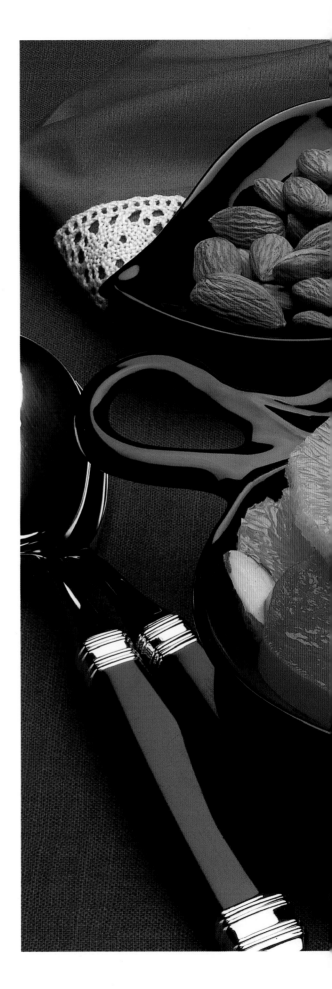

The sheltered waters in the Bay of Islands, Northland.

DESSERTS

New Zealand's most famous dessert was developed for a Russian ballerina, Pavlova, who visited the country in 1926. The recipe for the egg white based dessert was probably derived from the French meringue cake. There are many variations of the Pavlova, however, the most popular has a crisp outside and is marshmallow inside.

Many of our other desserts are based on local fruits such as tamarillos, strawberries, kiwifruit, feijoas, persimmon, passionfruit, kiwanos and assorted berries.

Eating ice cream is a national past time. Our creamy milk produces excellent ice cream and has become a snack food for young and old. Home-made ice creams using local fruits, vegetables and herbs have become fashionable and many restaurants feature unusual flavours.

Desserts from other countries such as strudels, tortes and gateaux have become part of the national cuisine.

PAVLOVA :above

2 egg whites
1½ cups caster (powdered) sugar
½ teaspoon vanilla essence
1 teaspoon white vinegar
1 teaspoon cornflour (cornstarch)
4 tablespoons boiling water

Topping: 1¼ cups cream
1 tablespoon icing (confectioners') sugar
sliced kiwifruit, strawberries, etc.

Place first six ingredients into a medium sized bowl and beat with a rotary or electric beater until mixture is smooth, shiny and stiff—about 12 minutes. Meanwhile place a sheet of greaseproof paper on a baking tray. Brush lightly with melted butter and dust with a little cornflour—shake off excess. Spoon meringue mixture onto prepared tray forming a 23 cm (9") circle. Bake in middle of oven, 180°C (350°F) for 10 minutes, reduce heat to 150°C (300°F) and bake a further 45 minutes. Allow to cool in oven. Whip cream with icing sugar until stiff. Spread on top of cooled pavlova. Top with fruit.

Serves about 6

Southern Rata in the Hollyford Valley, Fiordland.

WARM BERRY PIE

1 kg (2 lb) ripe blackberries, raspberries,
    blueberries or strawberries
juice 1 lemon
¼ cup port
¼ cup sugar
¼ cup flour
½ teaspoon ground cinnamon
400 g (14 oz) flaky pastry
25 g (1 oz) butter
1 tablespoon sugar, extra

Wash and drain berries if need be. Pour lemon juice and port over the fruit. Combine sugar, flour and cinnamon. Add to berries and turn fruit to coat in mixture. Line a 20 cm (8") pie plate with thinly rolled pastry. Trim. Spoon in the fruit. Dot with butter. Using off-cuts of pastry cut into strips and make a lattice weave pattern over the fruit. Sprinkle with sugar.

Bake at 200°C (400°F) for 35 minutes. Serve warm but not hot, with whipped cream.

Serves 6

PASSIONFRUIT CREPES :above

Crèpes: ½ cup flour
¼ teaspoon salt
4 teaspoons sugar
2 eggs
¾ cup milk
1 tablespoon oil
butter for frying

Topping: pulp of 6 passionfruit
2–3 tablespoons sugar

To make crèpes, sift dry ingredients into a bowl. Beat eggs and add to dry ingredients with milk and oil. Pour into a jug and stand for 2 hours. Heat a small amount of butter in a small heavy frypan. Pour about 3 tablespoons of batter into the pan and swirl around. Cook until golden then flip over. Cook until golden. Spoon a little sweetened passionfruit pulp over the crèpe and serve.

Serves about 4

FEIJOA SOUFFLE :above

    3 teaspoons powdered gelatine
    ¼ cup water
    2 cups feijoa pulp
    ¾ cup sugar
    2 tablespoons lemon juice
    2 egg whites
    1 cup cream, whipped
    ½ cup finely chopped nuts

Soak gelatine in water for 5 minutes then dissolve over hot water. Stir into feijoa pulp with sugar and lemon juice.

Whip egg whites until stiff then fold into pulp with whipped cream. Pour into a soufflé dish fitted with a paper collar. Refrigerate until set. Carefully remove the collar and dust sides of soufflé with nuts.

The top may be garnished with twists of feijoa and julienne of orange.

Serves 6–8

St James station horses and Spenser Mountains (near Lewis Pass).

TAMARILLO AND WALNUT ICE CREAM

2 cups peeled and sliced red tamarillos
¼ cup caster (powdered) sugar
2 teaspoons powdered gelatine
2 tablespoons water
75 g (3 oz) walnuts
1¼ cups cream
2 tablespoons caster (powdered) sugar, extra

Place prepared tamarillos into a small saucepan and spinkle with quarter cup caster sugar. Stand 15 minutes then bring to the boil. Cook 1 minute. Purée in a food processor or blender. Sieve to remove seeds. Soften gelatine in water. Dissolve over hot water and add to the purée. Cool. Chop walnuts coarsely and lightly toast in the oven at 180°C (350°F) for about 5 minutes. Cool.

Whip cream until thick. Fold in caster sugar, then the purée and nuts. Pour into a suitable container. Freeze until almost set, beat until light, then freeze again until firm.

Serves 4–5

MARINATED PEACHES IN
STRAWBERRY PUREE :above

820 g (1 lb 11 oz) can sliced peaches
¼ cup orange juice
2 tablespoons Galliano liqueur
2 cups strawberries

Garnish: mint leaves or violets

Drain the peach slices and trim to make even. Sprinkle juice and liqueur over the peaches and allow to marinate for about an hour.

Reserve 6 strawberries and purée remainder in a food processor or blender. Chill the mixture.

Spoon 3–4 tablespoons of purée on a large plate, arrange a few peach slices on top and garnish with reserved strawberries and mint or violets.

Serves 4–6

72

APPLE CHEESECAKE WITH LOGANBERRY COULIS :above

Loganberry Coulis: 2½ cups loganberries
3 tablespoons icing (confectioners') sugar
squeeze lemon juice

Cheesecake Crust: 250 g (8 oz) plain sweet
  biscuits
125 g (4 oz) butter, melted
pinch cinnamon

Cheesecake Filling: 2 large apples
¾ cup sugar
2 tablespoons powdered gelatine
½ cup warm water
500 g (1 lb) ricotta cheese
1 tablespoon lemon juice
1 tablespoon lemon zest
3 eggs, separated
2 tablespoons white wine
1 cup softly beaten cream

Purée loganberries, sugar and lemon juice together in a blender or food processor. Strain to remove seeds and chill until needed. To make the crust, crush biscuits finely, combine biscuit crumbs, melted butter and cinnamon, mix well. Spread over base and sides of well-greased 20 cm (8") cake tin with a loose base. Chill in refrigerator until set.

To make the filling, cook the apples with 1 tablespoon of sugar and a ¼ cup of water. Soften, then dissolve gelatine in the warm water. Purée the apples until smooth, add the gelatine and let the mixture stand to cool. Whisk the ricotta cheese with the lemon juice and zest until smooth. Place egg yolks, rest of sugar and wine in a double boiler and whisk until mixture becomes thick and creamy.

Combine the egg mixture with the ricotta, and then the apple purée. Fold in the whipped cream, then the stiffly beaten egg whites. Pour filling into prepared pie crust. Chill thoroughly before serving.

Serves 8

73

A Kotuku (white heron) at Milford Sound.

SPICY KUMARA PIE

2 eggs
½ cup sugar
½ cup golden syrup (treacle)
I cup mashed cooked kumara
I teaspoon ground ginger
I teaspoon ground cinnamon
½ teaspoon ground nutmeg
I cup milk
23 cm (9") baked pie shell

Beat eggs well, adding sugar and golden syrup slowly. Add well-mashed kumara with spices and milk. Pour in the baked pie shell and bake at 180°C (350°F) for 45 minutes until filling is set. Cover loosely with foil if pastry browns too much. Serve warm or at room temperature with whipped cream.

Serves 6

PEAR AND ALMOND FLAN :above

Pastry: 1¼ cups flour
100 g (3½ oz) butter, softened
3 tablespoons caster (powdered) sugar
1 egg

Filling: ½ cup sugar
2 cups water
3 firm pears
50 g (2 oz) butter
75 g (3 oz) caster (powered) sugar
½ teaspoon finely grated lemon rind
2 eggs
1 cup ground almonds
¼ cup semolina
2 tablespoons lemon juice
25 g (1 oz) blanched almonds

To prepare pastry, mix all ingredients in a food processor to form a dough. Otherwise knead mixture by hand. Wrap dough in plastic film and refrigerate for at least 30 minutes. Preheat oven to 180°C (350°F).

Roll out pastry on a lightly floured surface. Line a 25 cm (10") flan tin.

To prepare filling, heat sugar and water until dissolved. Bring to the boil. Peel, quarter and core pears and simmer in syrup until tender. Drain pears.

Cream butter, caster sugar and lemon rind. Beat in eggs one at a time. Combine ground almonds and semolina. Fold into creamed mixture. Finally mix in lemon juice. Spread filling into pastry case. Arrange drained pears and almonds over filling. Bake at 180°C (350°F) for 30–35 minutes or until filling is set and golden brown. Serve warm. Flan may be glazed with warmed apple jelly

Serves 6–8

Warbrick Terrace at Waimangu thermal reserve, Rotorua.

LEMON DELICIOUS PUDDING

25 g (1 oz) butter
1 cup sugar
2 tablespoons flour
¼ cup lemon juice
3 teaspoons grated lemon rind
2 eggs
1 cup milk

Soften the butter and beat in the sugar, the flour, lemon juice and grated lemon rind. Separate the eggs. Beat the egg yolks and milk together and stir into the mixture. Beat the egg white until stiff and fold in.

Pour into a 3½ cup capacity baking dish. Set in a pan of water in the oven. Bake at 160°C (325°F) for 1 hour.

Serves 6

RASPBERRIES IN AN ALMOND BISCUIT WITH RASPBERRY CREAM :above

Almond Cornets:
1 egg
¼ cup caster (powdered) sugar)
few drops vanilla essence
25 g (1 oz) ground almonds
½ cup flour
pinch salt
2 tablespoons cream

2×250 g (9 oz) punnets raspberries

Raspberry Cream:
¼ cup icing (confectioners') sugar
2 teaspoons powdered gelatine
250 g (9 oz) cream cheese

Cream the egg, sugar and vanilla. Add the ground almonds, then stir in the flour and salt. Cover and refrigerate for at least 1 hour. Grease and flour a baking tray. Using a small plate 12 cm (4") in diameter, trace circles into the flour on the tray so the biscuits will be an even consistent shape. Once the batter has rested, take from the refrigerator and stir in the cream.

Spread the batter thinly within the marked circles on the baking tray. Bake at 180°C (350°F) for about 5 minutes or until the edges of the biscuits begin to brown. Working quickly while the biscuits are still warm, twist them around the handle of a wooden spoon or a cream-horn mould. Cool on a wire rack. Fill with fresh raspberries and garnish with raspberry cream.

To make the raspberry cream, take the second punnet of raspberries, and purée in a food processor. Strain to remove the seeds, bring to the boil with the icing sugar. Remove from heat, add the gelatine and stir until dissolved. Cool. In the food processor whisk the cream cheese and raspberry purée until smooth. Lastly add the cream and whisk very briefly to combine. Allow to chill thoroughly before serving.

Makes 15 cornets.

Pleasure craft at Lake Taupo boat harbour.

CAKES AND BAKES

The first recipes for baking were brought to this country by settlers from England. Scones, pikelets, shortbread, fruit cakes, have all stood the test of time and are still prepared at home and commercially.

A few items are kiwi originals such as Kiwi Crisps and Anzac biscuits. Others have been developed with the products of the countryside. Apple, grapefruit and tangelo cakes use produce typical to New Zealand.

The health trend has influenced the country's cooking—bran muffins, wholemeal cakes and muesli biscuits are a feature. But at the opposite end of the scale chocolate cakes have never been as popular.

Often now used as a sweet ending to meals, cakes and cookies will always be part of the New Zealand diet.

SPICY APPLE CAKE :above

1½ cups apple, peeled, cored and chopped
½ cup brown sugar
½ cup sticky raisins
½ cup chopped walnuts
½ cup instant non-fat dried milk
1 cup wholemeal flour
1 cup flour
2½ teaspoons baking powder
½ teaspoon salt
2 teaspoons ground cinnamon
2 teaspoons mixed spice
50 g (2 oz) butter
2 eggs
250 ml (9 fl oz) packet apple juice

Place apple and brown sugar in a large bowl. Allow to stand 5 minutes. Add raisins, walnuts, milk and wholemeal flour. Sift flour, baking powder, salt, cinnamon and mixed spice. Add to the apple mixture and mix well. Melt butter and mix with eggs and apple juice in a bowl, beating well. Stir into the dry ingredients without over mixing.

Turn into a greased round cake tin 20 cm (8") in diameter.

Bake at 200°C (400°F) for 45 minutes or until golden brown and an inserted skewer comes out clean. Cool in tin for 15 minutes before removing.

Lake Middleton and the Barrier Range, South Canterbury.

OAT BRAN AND GINGER SLICES

½ cup oil
¾ cup raw sugar
50 g (2 oz) crystalised ginger, thinly sliced
1 teaspoon ground cinnamon
¾ cup oat bran
1 egg, lightly beaten
1 cup flour
½ teaspoon baking powder

Heat oil and sugar in a heavy based saucepan over a low heat. Stir in ginger and cinnamon. Remove from heat. Stir in the oat bran and beaten egg. Finally mix in the flour and baking powder. Stir thoroughly. Press into prepared 20 cm (8") tin. Prick the surface with a fork. Bake at 180°C (350°F) for 20–25 minutes. While still warm, mark into wedges. Allow to cool in tin.

Makes about 16.

SESAME CHEESE STICKS :above

    ¾ cup stone ground wholemeal flour
    ¾ cup white flour
    ¼ teaspoon salt (optional)
    2 teaspoons baking powder
    ¼ cup sesame seeds
    125 g (4 oz) butter, cubed
    175 g (6 oz) cheese, cubed
    4–5 tablespoons milk

  Preheat oven to 190°C (375°F). In a food processor bowl, combine the dry ingredients and sesame seeds. Add the butter and cheese. Process for about 20 seconds or until the mixture is crumbly. Add milk. Process to form a dough. Roll out dough to 3 mm (⅛") thickness. Cut into stick shapes about 10 cm (4") long and 2 cm (¾") wide.

  Place on oven trays. Bake at 200°C (400°F) for about 8 minutes or until golden brown.

Makes about 48.

Beech forest on the Keplar Track, Fiordland National Park.

TRADITIONAL FRUIT CAKE :left

400 g (14 oz) sultanas
500 g (1 lb) raisins
125 g (4 oz) currants
150 g (5 oz) glacé cherries
150 g (5 oz) mixed peel
½ cup brandy or sherry
225 g (8 oz) butter
1½ cups brown sugar, firmly packed
1 teaspoon grated orange rind
1 teaspoon grated lemon rind
⅛ teaspoon almond essence
1 teaspoon vanilla essence
2 tablespoons marmalade
1 teaspoon caramel essence
4 eggs
2½ cups flour
pinch salt
1 teaspoon mixed spice
¼ teaspoon each ground cinnamon, nutmeg

Chop fruits and place in a large bowl. Pour over brandy and mix well. Cover and stand overnight.

Prepare a 20 cm (8") round cake pan, line with two thickness brown paper and one of greaseproof.

Cream butter and sugar until light and fluffy. Add fruit rinds, essences and marmalades.

Drop eggs in one at a time, beating well after each addition. If the mixture starts to curdle, add a little of the flour. Fold in prepared fruits alternately with sifted dry ingredients. Mix well. Pour into a lined tin. Smooth over the top with a wet hand. Bake at 150°C (300°F) or about 3 hours or until a skewer inserted in the centre comes out clean. Remove cake from pan, cool and wrap in foil to store.

ANZAC BISCUITS

¼ cup sugar
½ cup flour
¾ cup desiccated coconut
½ cup rolled oats
50 g (2 oz) butter
1 tablespoon golden syrup (treacle)
½ teaspoon baking soda
2 tablespoons boiling water

Combine sugar, flour, coconut and rolled oats in a large bowl. Melt butter and syrup on low heat. Dissolve soda in boiling water and add to butter mixture. Make a well in the centre of the dry ingredients and stir in the liquid. Mix well.

Place in spoonfuls on a lightly greased tray. Bake at 180°C (350°F) for about 15 minutes. Remove from tray with a spatula and allow to cool on a wire rack. Store in an airtight container.

Makes about 12.

83

Whakamahi Beach, Wairoa.

TANGELO AND POPPY SEED CAKE

250 g (9 oz) light cream cheese
125 g (4 oz) butter
1 cup sugar
3 eggs, separated
2 cups flour
1 teaspoon baking powder
1 teaspoon baking soda
1 cup low fat yoghurt
2 tablespoons poppy seeds
1 tablespoon grated tangelo rind

Topping: ½ cup sugar
⅓ cup orange liqueur
¼ cup tangelo juice
3 tablespoons icing (confectioners') sugar

Beat cream cheese,, butter and the 1 cup sugar until smooth and well blended. Add egg yolks one at a time mixing well after each addition. Sift flour, baking powder and baking soda. Add to cream cheese mixture alternately with yoghurt. Stir in poppy seeds and peel. Beat egg whites until stiff. Fold into cream cheese mixture.

Pour into a 25 cm (10") ring pan. Bake 50 minutes at 180°C (350°F).

Stir the ½ cup sugar, liqueur and juice in a saucepan over low heat until sugar dissolves.

Prick hot cake several times with a skewer. Pour syrup over cake. Stand for 10 minutes. Invert onto a serving plate. Cool completely. Sprinkle with icing sugar before serving.

Makes about 16 slices.

PIKELETS :above

2 cups sifted flour
3 teaspoons baking powder
1 teaspoon salt
2 eggs
2 tablespoons sugar
25 g (1 oz) butter
1¼ cups milk

Sift dry ingredients into mixing bowl. Beat eggs and sugar. Combine melted butter and milk and pour into egg mixture. Add to flour, stirring only enough to moisten ingredients.

Place dessertspoons of the mixture on a lightly greased hot frypan or griddle. Cook until bubbles appear on topside then turn over to cook on other side.

Makes about 20 pikelets.

Wanganui River near Jerusalem.

KIWI CRISPS

125 g (4 oz) butter
50 g (2 oz) sugar
1 tablespoon sweetened condensed milk
¼ teaspoon vanilla essence
175 g (6 oz) flour
1 teaspoon baking powder
50 g (2 oz) chocolate chips

Cream butter, sugar and condensed milk. Add essence. Sift flour and baking powder and add to creamed mixture. Stir in chocolate chips. Roll mixture into small balls and place on a greased oven tray. Flatten balls with a fork. Bake at 180°C (350°F) for approximately 20 minutes.

Makes about 15.

CRUNCHY APPLE MUFFINS :above

Topping: ¼ cup brown sugar
¼ cup chopped pecan nuts or walnuts
½ teaspoon ground cinnamon
2 teaspoons butter

Muffins: I egg
½ cup milk
50 g (2 oz) butter, melted
¼ cup brown sugar
I cup flour
I teaspoon baking powder
¼ teaspoon baking soda
I teaspoon ground cinnamon
½ cup oat bran
250 g (9oz) apples, peeled and grated

Preheat oven to 200°C (400°F). Lightly grease the muffin pans.

To prepare topping, mix all ingredients until crumbly. To prepare the muffins, beat together the egg, milk, butter and sugar. In a separate bowl, sift the flour, baking powder, baking soda and cinnamon. Stir in the oat bran and grated apple. Stir the liquid ingredients into the apple mixture until just combined.

Placed heaped tablespoons of the mixture in each muffin pan. Sprinkle over topping. Bake for 18–20 minutes or until evenly browned. Remove muffins from oven. Allow to cool in the muffin pans for 2–3 minutes. Serve warm with butter.

Makes I2 medium sized muffins.

87

Farm homestead in the hill country near Taihape.

BEER, WINE AND CHEESE

The New Zealand wine industry was first started in the mid-nineteenth century by immigrants from Yugoslavia. Our wine industry has gone from strength to strength and today our wines win awards around the world. There are several different vine growing areas in the country (see map) many specialising in varietal grapes and wines.

The brewing of beer is highly commercialised in this country with two major brewers. Both companies export beer worldwide. However, there are many small boutique breweries throughout the country. The beers have a character all of their own.

Cheeses of this country are highly sophisticated. With such an abundance of dairy milk it is little wonder that cheeses also win awards overseas. Over the years, many of the large cheesemakers have diversified into exotic lines. Camembert, Brie, Parmesan, fetta, gruyere, as well as some kiwi names such as Kahurangi and Kapati, are but just a few of the variety of cheeses. There are also small cheesemakers in just about every province, many of European origin, producing continental-style cheeses with a unique kiwi flavour.

MAJOR VINEYARD AREAS

Kumeu
Henderson • • Auckland
Te Kauwhata • Tauranga

Gisborne •

Napier
• Hastings

Martinborough

Nelson
• Blenheim

Christchurch

Central Otago

CHEESE MUFFINS :above

2 cups flour
4 teaspoons baking powder
1 tablespoon sugar
1 teaspoon salt
1 cup shredded cheddar cheese
2 eggs, lightly beaten
1 cup milk
2 tablespoons melted butter
extra shredded cheese for garnish

Sift flour, baking powder, sugar and salt into a large bowl. Reserve a little cheese for the tops. Add remaining cheese and mix well. Combine eggs with milk and butter. Add liquid ingredients to the dry, stirring just enough to wet the mixture. Do not over mix.

Take heaped spoonfuls and fill 8–10 greased muffin pans. Sprinkle with reserved cheese. Bake at 220°C (425°F) for 12–15 minutes in the centre of the oven. Cool 5 minutes before removing from pans.

Makes 8–10 medium muffins.

Taranaki farmland and Mt Egmont.

BEER BATTERED ASPARAGUS

1 cup flour
½ teaspoon salt
1 teaspoon paprika
370 ml (13 fl oz) beer
1 kg (2 lb) asparagus
oil for deep frying

Sift flour, salt and paprika. Whisk in sufficient beer to make a thin batter. This may be used immediately or stored in a covered container in the refrigerator. Prepare asparagus as for cooking. Lightly dust with flour.

Heat about 5 cm (2") of oil in a heavy frypan, wide enough to take the asparagus. Stir batter then dip asparagus into batter and lower carefully into the oil. Cook until golden, about 2 minutes, turning carefully with a slotted spoon. Do not fry too many spears at once as the temperature of the oil will drop.

Drain on absorbent paper. Keep warm in oven while remainder cook. Serve immediately as a starter, or a cocktail or main course accompaniment.

90

Serves about 6

HERBED YOGHURT CHEESE SERVED
WITH FRESH GRAPES :above

4 cups (1 litre) natural unsweetened
  yoghurt
2 tablespoons each chopped fresh chives,
  thyme and marjoram
1–2 teaspoons sugar
⅓ cup of lightly roasted chopped walnuts
salt and pepper

Line a strainer with fine muslin then place the
strainer over a bowl to collect the whey. Pour the
yoghurt into the strainer and leave to drain in the
refrigerator for at least 48 hours. Take the cheese from
the strainer and discard the whey. Blend the chives,
thyme and marjoram into the cheese. Season with
sugar to reduce the tartness if desired. Add salt and
pepper to taste.

Roll in freshly chopped herbs and lightly roasted
chopped walnuts. Serve with fresh grapes and French
bread.

Serves 4

Southern Alps from Lake Mapourika, Westland.

CHAMPAGNE AND GRAPES :above

8–12 grapes will be required for each serving. Deseed the grapes and marinate in good quality brut Champagne. Leave in the refrigerator at least 2 hours. Recork the rest of the Champagne and keep chilled. Take some further small neat bunches of 4–5 grapes and brush each bunch with lightly beaten white of one egg, making sure they are completely covered.

Dip into caster (powdered) sugar. Shake off excess and check the grapes are completely covered. Place on a tray and leave to stand for 2–3 hours in a dry place.

To serve, fill champagne flutes with the macerated grapes. Fill the glasses with Champagne. Garnish with the frosted grapes and a sprig of mint.

SANGRIA

¼ cup sugar
¾ cup water
750 ml (24 fl oz) bottle soft red wine
I orange, thinly sliced
I lime, thinly sliced
I lemon, thinly sliced
I cup soda water

Dissolve the sugar in the water in a large jug. Add the wine and fruit and refrigerate for an hour. Before serving add the soda water and some ice cubes.

Serves 6–8

KIR :above

Pronounced "kea". A famous French drink prepared with New Zealand ingredients. Serve well chilled in summer.

> 1 part crème de cassis (blackcurrant liqueur)
> 4–5 parts chilled white wine

Pour Cassis in a wine glass and top up with a good medium or dry white wine.

INDEX

We would like to acknowledge the assistance of all the above named individuals and companies who have supplied recipes and photographs.